A Field Guide to the
Reptiles and Amphibians
of Coastal Southern California

By

Robert N. Fisher

and

Ted J. Case

Department of Biology-0116
University of California at San Diego
La Jolla, Ca 92093-0116

*The authors thank our wives and families
for their support and patience over the years*

Copyright © 1997 by Robert N. Fisher and Ted J. Case.

ISBN 0-9660059-0-2

Library of Congress Catalog Card Number: 97-92514

Published in 1997

Sponsored by the Biological Resources Division of the United States Geological Service

Printed in the United States by Lazer Touch, San Mateo, CA

Contents

Introduction	2
Acknowledgements/Picture Credits	3
Species Lists	4
Range Map	6
Species Accounts	
Salamanders	7
Frogs and Toads	11
Tadpoles	17
Turtles	18
Lizards	20
Snakes	32
Glossary of terms	44

View of coastal sage scrub habitat in Camp Pendelton, San Diego Co., California

A Field Guide to the Reptiles and Amphibians of Coastal Southern California

Introduction

While there are several excellent field guides that cover identification of reptiles and amphibians in the United States, the striking geographic variation, occasional sexual dimorphism, and developmental changes of species over this large geographic range can confuse identification. The highly developed and urbanized area of coastal Southern California is host to one of the richest herpetofaunas in the United States and includes several species with State and Federal protected status. Over the past few years, we have been conducting an intensive study of the autecology of herptile communities in the region and saw the pressing need for a well-illustrated field guide to help train students, researchers, reserve managers, regulators, and others to identify the local herpetofauna, with emphasis on sensitive species. We recognized this need in the wake of a proliferation of environmental documents (gray literature) and reviews dealing with many species that are either poorly known or commonly misidentified. Our goal is that this guide, by aiding in the correct identification of species, will increase the understanding of this group and the utility of biology work currently underway in southern California. As this project progressed it became clear that by covering all the species, including very localized ones, we would appeal to a larger audience and hopefully spawn interest in this very diverse, threatened fauna. This fauna is especially rich due to the co-occurrence of mountain, desert, scrub, and Baja elements in the heterogeneous habitat available on the coastal slope. This book includes all the species that are native in the geographic focal area (see map, page 6). Subspecies are included as well, when they may be distinguished by characters in the field (e.g. the California mountain kingsnake and red racer). We do not attempt to distinguish the subspecies of the western skink or the ring-necked snake. This choice is not meant to imply any taxonomic reanalysis (although this may be called for in the future). Introduced species are included if they are relatively widespread and seem to have self-sustaining natural populations. For example, we have excluded *Anolis* and desert tortoises. The former is distributed in the immediate vicinity of the San Diego Zoo and the latter shows up as occasional escaped pets. Marine and island species were not included in this guide.

The format for the guide is to present a color photograph of each species, for which we tried to obtain a photo of a local specimen. The photos are accompanied with the following information to aid in identification:

Scientific name: Based on our understanding of the current nomenclature of the species; subspecies names are included when they can be distinguished in the field.
Common name: The name used follows Robert Stebbin's 1985 "A field guide to western reptiles and amphibians" (Houghton Mifflin Company).
Four letter species code: This is usually the first two letters of the genus and species. We are using these codes in our research and feel it is important to try to standardize them locally.
Distribution within study area: This is a general summary of the distribution of a species within the focal area (see map, page 6) based on our observations, museum records, or other literature records.
Size: We present the minimum and maximum adult snout to vent lengths for all species except for turtles for which we present carapace lengths. The measurements we present are based on the literature and unpublished data we and Dan Holland have been collecting for the last two years. In some instances we have measurements for 1,000+ individuals of a species and where we differ from the literature we have used our data.
Distinguishing characters: We have tried to provide simple visual characteristics to help identify the species in our region. We have tried to make the terminology as non-technical as possible but still found it necessary to include a glossary of diagrams in the back of the book to illustrate characteristics with which readers may be unfamiliar.
Juveniles: If there are any obvious ontogenetic changes in the species, then we describe them here. We present a page of tadpole illustrations to help in their identification, located after the section on frogs and toads.
Dimorphism: If there are known obvious morphological differences between the sexes in a species, then these are described in this section.

Similar species: We describe characters that are useful in telling similar looking species apart, especially if these species occur in sympatry.

Additional notes: In this section we briefly point out distributional restrictions, natural history observations, or behavioral traits of a species or subspecies.

The order of species in the book does not necessarily reflect taxonomic or phylogenetic relationships, but rather is based on general similarity in appearance. Species which are most often confused are kept close together in the book.

Acknowledgments

Tiffany Garcia, then at UC Davis, initiated the first PageMaker file as an independent research project under the review of Brad Shaffer. In conjunction with our extensive field work, we noted many differences in the body sizes and appearance of local forms compared to those generally illustrated in other field guides. Bob Haase and Chris Brown had been working with students and volunteers on our project, and their experience working with both neophytes and trained colleagues was invaluable to refining the identification scheme. As our field study on local populations progressed, the field guide project also expanded in coverage with the addition of about one third more species. The vast majority of the photographs were taken by Dan Holland, many specifically for this project. Dan also drew the figure showing the side views of the tadpoles and he advised us on species accounts based on his extensive studies at Camp Pendleton. Jon Richmond drew all the illustrations for the glossary and the dorsal views of the tadpoles. Many of these drawings were adapted from Robert Stebbin's 1985 "A field guide to western reptiles and amphibians". Greg Nichols of the US Department of Forestry created the GIS map. Review of many of the species accounts was done by Ed Ervin, Paul Griffin, Kathy Klingenberg, Andy Suarez, and Marie Vicario.

Our field research was supported by the Metropolitan Water District of California, the Biological Resources Division of USGS, the California Department of Fish and Game, the California State Parks Department, US Fish and Wildlife Service, US Department of Forestry, and the National Science Foundation. Special thanks go to Peter Stine at the Biological Resources Division of USGS for his support of the project from its inception.

We also want to thank the many students at the University of California at San Diego, San Diego State University, the University of San Diego, the University of California at Irvine, Cal Poly Pomona, and other colleges who helped us in the field and laboratory. Special thanks also go to Stacie Hathaway and the docents of Torrey Pines State Reserve, and Samantha Weber and the volunteers at Cabrillo National Monument for their help. Peter Bowler, John Stephenson, Lisa Underwood, Greg Pregill, Andy Yuen, Bill Tippits, Bill Wagner, Eddy Konno, Jud Monroe, Mike Wells, Liam Davis, Gail Kobetich, John Bradley, Mark Pavelka, Steve Viers, Tom Oberbauer, Slader Buck, Rick Griffiths, Pat Mock, Isabelle Kay, Barbara Carlson, John Rotenberry, Mike Hamilton, Don Lydy, Jeff Opdycke, Trish Smith, Sedra Shapiro, Mike Mitchell, Joe Funk, Larry Smith, Joel Chew, Pete DeSimone, Geary Hund, Ed Camp....and many others were instrumental in cementing logistics.

We also express our appreciation to the San Diego Natural History Museum, the Los Angeles County Museum, the Museum of Vertebrate Zoology, and the California Academy of Sciences for loans and information from their collections.

Photographs used from sources other than Dan Holland are acknowledged below using the species codes: Shane Bagnall: SCGR (left); Pete Bloom: AREL (top right); Chris Brown: MAFU (left), URMI (underside); Ed Ervin: MAFU (right); Robert Goodman, Jr.: CHBO (all three); Mark Jennings: RAMU (both); Mark Lempke: CRVE (both); Brad Shaffer: AMTI (all three), LITR (top right), RACA (left), SCMA; John Tashjian: BAPA (right), COVA (left), GACO; Wayne VanDevender: PHXA, URMI (left); Bill Wagner: BUPU; Dave Wake: ENKL (large one).

Species found in coastal southern California and included in Guide
Native Species

Salamanders

Plethodontidae — Page number
- *Aneides lugubris* — 7
- *Batrachoseps gabrieli* — 7
- *Batrachoseps nigriventris* — 8
- *Batrachoseps pacificus major* — 8
- *Ensatina eschscholtzii eschscholtzii* — 9
- *Ensatina eschscholtzii klauberi* * — 9

Salamandridae
- *Taricha torosa* * — 10

Frogs

Bufonidae
- *Bufo boreas* — 11
- *Bufo microscaphus californicus* * — 11
- *Bufo punctatus* — 12

Hylidae
- *Hyla cadaverina* — 13
- *Hyla regilla* — 13

Pelobatidae
- *Scaphiopus (Spea) hammondii* * — 12

Ranidae
- *Rana aurora draytoni* * — 14
- *Rana boylii* * — 15
- *Rana muscosa* * — 15

Turtles

Emydidae
- *Clemmys marmorata* * — 18

Lizards

Anguidae
- *Elgaria multicarinatus* — 20

Anniellidae
- *Anniella pulchra* * — 20

Crotaphytidae
- *Crotaphytus bicinctores* — 25
- *Crotaphytus vestigium* — 25
- *Gambelia copei* — 26
- *Gambelia wislizenii* — 26

Gekkonidae
- *Coleonyx variegatus abbotti* * — 23
- *Phyllodactylus xanti* * — 23

Phrynosomatidae
- *Callisaurus draconoides* — 28
- *Petrosaurus mearnsi* — 28
- *Phrynosoma coronatum* * — 27
- *Phrynosoma platyrhinos* — 27
- *Sceloporus graciosus* * — 29
- *Sceloporus magister* — 30
- *Sceloporus occidentalis* — 29
- *Sceloporus orcutti* — 30
- *Urosaurus microscutatus (nigricaudus)* — 31
- *Uta stansburiana* — 31

Scincidae
- *Eumeces gilberti* — 22
- *Eumeces skiltonianus* * — 22

Teiidae — Page number
- *Cnemidophorus hyperythrus* * — 21
- *Cnemidophorus tigris* * — 21

Xantusidae
- *Xantusia henshawi* * — 24
- *Xantusia vigilis* — 24

Snakes

Boidae
- *Charina bottae* * — 32
- *Charina (Lichanura) trivirgata* * — 32

Colubridae
- *Arizona elegans* — 33
- *Coluber constrictor* — 35
- *Diadophis punctatus* * — 34
- *Hypsiglena torquata* — 41
- *Lampropeltis getula* — 38
- *Lampropeltis zonata parvirubra* * — 39
- *Lampropeltis zonata pulchra* * — 39
- *Masticophis flagellum fuliganosus* — 36
- *Masticophis flagellum piceus* — 36
- *Masticophis lateralis* — 37
- *Pituophis melanoleucus* — 33
- *Rhinocheilus lecontei* — 38
- *Salvadora hexalepis* * — 37
- *Tantilla planiceps* — 34
- *Thamnophis elegans* — 40
- *Thamnophis hammondii* * — 35
- *Thamnophis sirtalis* * — 40
- *Trimorphodon biscutatus* — 41

Leptotyphlopidae
- *Leptotyphlops humilis* — 43

Viperidae
- *Crotalus mitchellii* — 43
- *Crotalus ruber (exsul)* * — 42
- *Crotalus viridis* — 42

Introduced Species

Salamanders

Ambystomatidae
- *Ambystoma tigrinum* — 10

Frogs

Pipidae
- *Xenopus laevis* — 16

Ranidae
- *Rana catesbeiana* — 16
- *Rana pipiens* complex — 14

Turtles

Chelydridae
- *Chelydra serpentina* — 19

Emydidae
- *Trachemys scripta* — 18

Trionychidae
- *Apalone spinifera* — 19

* Indicates species officially considered sensitive or protected.

Species found in coastal southern California and not included in Field Guide*

Island Species

Salamanders
Plethodontidae
Batrachoseps pacificus pacificus

Lizards
Xantusidae
Xantusia riversiana

Marine Species

Turtles
Cheloniidae
Caretta caretta
Chelonia mydas
Eretmochelys imbricata
Lepidochelys olivacea
Dermochelyidae
Dermochelys coriacea

Snakes
Hydrophiidae
Pelamis platurus

* The field guide only included terrestrial species on the mainland.

View of ocean over coastal sage scrub, San Diego Co., California

Coastal Southern California Topography

The study region extends from the Mexican Border north to the Sierra Pelona Mountains, from the ocean to the crest of the mountains. This incorporates portions of Los Angeles, Orange, Riverside, San Bernardino, and San Diego Counties.

Juvenile

Scientific name: *Aneides lugubris*   **Common name:** Arboreal Salamander
Four letter species code: ANLU   **Distribution within study area:** All regions, except eastern Riverside and
Size: 2.2-3.2 in (5.6-8.1 cm)   San Bernardino Counties.
Distinguishing characters: A large species with plain purplish-brown coloring usually spotted dorsally with gold or yellow, although may be unspotted; large, triangular shaped head; large squared off toes.
Juveniles: Dark overall; clouded with greyish color and fine yellow speckling on back; rust markings on snout, along tail and on sides above forelimbs.
Dimorphism: Male has a broad triangular shaped head, with the front teeth of the jaw extend beyond the bottom lip.
Similar species: *Ensatina e. eschscholtzii*: Has lighter overall coloration; lacks dorsal spotting; head less distinct from neck.
Taricha torosa: Lacks yellow spots and has rough, warty skin with a vertical flat tail. *Ensatina e. klauberi*: Has tail constriction; generally larger yellow blotches.
Additional notes: This species is an excellent climber and difficult to capture. Large adults can inflict a painful bite. Primarily associated with oak and sycamore woodlands, and thick chaparral.

Scientific name: *Batrachoseps gabrieli*   **Common name:** San Gabriel Mountain Slender Salamander
Four letter species code: BAGA   **Distribution within study area:** San Gabriel Canyon, Los Angeles County.
Size: 1.25-2.0 in (3.1-5.0 cm)
Distinguishing characters: A large species; worm-like body, large head and limbs; elongate cylindrical tail less than 1.5 times body length; black dorsum with white/coppery/orange blotches; immaculate black venter; may have red spots on tail.
Juveniles: Similar to adults.
Dimorphism: None
Similar species: *Batrachoseps pacificus*: Lacks white spots on dorsum; paler overall coloration. *Batrachoseps nigriventris*: Lacks white spots on dorsum, and has white dots on black underside.
Additional notes: Only known from San Gabriel Canyon system; typically above 1,000 meters in the San Gabriel Mountains of Los Angeles County.

Scientific name: *Batrachoseps nigriventris*
Four letter species code: BANI
Size: 1.22-1.70 in (3.1-4.3 cm)
Common name: Black-Bellied Slender Salamander
Distribution within study area: Los Angeles, Orange, western Riverside, and western San Bernardino Counties.
Distinguishing characters: A small species; worm-like body, small head and limbs; long cylindrical tail nearly twice body length; black, tan, reddish, brown or beige dorsum often with contrasting broad mid-dorsal stripe of similar colors; purplish or black venter with fine light speckling over entire surface.
Juveniles: Similar to adults; more pronounced dorsal stripe contrast in some individuals.
Dimorphism: None
Similar species: *Batrachoseps pacificus*: Has larger head, longer limbs; lacks dark venter with light speckling; paler overall coloration. High elevation (over 1,000 meters) *Batrachoseps pacificus* in San Diego Co. look very similar to *Batrachoseps nigriventris*. *Batrachoseps gabrieli*: Only occurs in San Gabriel Canyon, Los Angeles Co., has larger head and limbs than *Batrachoseps nigriventris*.
Additional notes: Occurs primarily southward to Orange County and northwestern Riverside County where it can be sympatric with *Batrachoseps pacificus*. This species will coil its body and tail when handled; it is fragile and easily injured. Prefers oak and sycamore woodlands over other habitats.

Scientific name: *Batrachoseps pacificus major*
Four letter species code: BAPA
Size: 1.30-2.64 in (3.3-6.7 cm)
Common name: Pacific Slender Salamander
Distribution within study area: Entire study area.
Distinguishing characters: A worm-like species with a long, slender body and tail; small head and limbs; highly variable coloration of brownish, light tan, pinkish or greyish dorsum with faint speckling on venter.
Juveniles: Similar to adults.
Dimorphism: None
Similar species: *Batrachoseps nigriventris*: Has narrower head; smaller, short limbs; distinct dorsal stripe; black venter; longer tail.
Additional notes: A common species throughout the study area with a complex evolutionary history; often coils body and tail tightly when handled; fragile and easily injured. Broadly distributed in many habitat types, including dry south-facing slopes.

Scientific name: *Ensatina eschscholtzii eschscholtzii*
Four letter species code: ENES
Size: 2.17-3.03 in (5.5-7.7 cm)
Common name: Monterey Salamander
Distribution within study area: All counties typically between 300 and 2,000 meters elevation.
Distinguishing characters: A moderate-sized species; reddish-brown dorsum with lighter venter; large, black eyes; smooth skin; swollen tail with a conspicuous constricted base.
Juveniles: Bright orange on dorsum, but generally similar to adults.
Dimorphism: Male has an enlarged upper lip; slimmer, longer tail that has a more pronounced constriction at the base.
Similar species: *Aneides lugubris*: Has broad, chunky head; yellow or gold dorsal spotting; lacks tail constriction at base. *Taricha torosa*: Has rough skin; laterally flattened tail, lacking constriction at base.
Additional notes: Uncommonly seen, but occurs in a variety of habitats especially within oak and coniferous woodlands, and chaparral within study area. Most active during and after rains. Docile and easily handled. May exude milky tail secretion that is toxic.

Scientific name: *Ensatina eschscholtzii klauberi*
Four letter species code: ENKL
Size: 2.17-3.15 in (5.5-8.0 cm)
Common name: Large-Blotched Salamander
Distribution within study area: High elevations (over 1,000 meters) of Riverside, San Bernardino, and San Diego Counties.
Distinguishing characters: A moderate-sized species; black or dark brown with orange or yellow transverse bands on dorsum of body and tail; large, black eyes; smooth skin; swollen tail with a conspicuous constricted base.
Juveniles: Similar to adults
Dimorphism: Male has an enlarged upper lip; slimmer, longer tail, with a more pronounced constriction at the tail base.
Similar species: *Aneides lugubris*: Has broad, chunky head; yellow or gold dorsal spotting. *Ensatina e. eschscholtzii*: Lacks the dorsal blotches.
Additional notes: Uncommonly seen; but occurs in localized, concentrated populations. Most active during and after rains. Docile and easily handled. Prefers oak and pine woodlands.

Scientific name: *Taricha torosa*
Four letter species code: TATO
Size: 2.75-3.5in (6.9-8.7 cm)
Common name: California Newt
Distribution within study area: Los Angeles, Orange, western Riverside, and San Diego Counties.

Distinguishing characters: A distinctive species with light-colored lower eyelids; light brown dorsum; reddish-orange or yellow venter; large eyes and rough skin; tail flattened laterally.
Juveniles: Similar to adults.
Dimorphism: Breeding males have flattened tail; dark skin on undersides of feet; smooth skin.
Similar species: *Ensatina e. eschscholtzii*: Has smooth skin; round tail with constricted base; black eyes. *Aneides lugubris*: Has smooth skin, and yellow spots.
Additional notes: Populations are localized within study area. Occurs along creeks and streams close to water, especially in rocky areas. Docile and easily handled, although skin secretions are toxic.

Scientific name: *Ambystoma tigrinum/californiense*
Four letter species code: AMTI
Size: 2.75-6.5 in (6.9-16.2 cm)
Common name: Tiger salamander
Distribution within study area: Introduced, generally near lakes.
INTRODUCED: Native to majority of U.S.

Distinguishing characters: A very large heavy bodied species with a rounded snout; coloration variable from uniform grey, to black and blotched; small eyes and smooth skin; tail flattened laterally.
Juveniles: Similar to adults, but dorsal pattern more diffuse.
Dimorphism: Breeding males have enlarged vent.
Similar species: All other native salamanders are much smaller and lack rounded snout.
Additional notes: May be localized within study area, as no reproducing populations are known. Individuals show up infrequently. This species and *Taricha torosa* are the only two salamanders in our focal area to have aquatic larvae.

BUBO tadpoles above, BUMI below.

Scientific name: *Bufo boreas*
Four letter species code: BUBO
Size: 2.2-5.12 in (5.6-13.0 cm)
Common name: Western Toad
Distribution within study area: Entire study area.

Distinguishing characters: A large toad species; white or cream dorsal stripe; dusky gray or greenish dorsally with skin glands concentrated within the dark blotches; parotoid glands are oval, widely separated, and larger than upper eyelids; mottled venter; horizontal pupils; lacks cranial crests.
Juveniles: Dorsal stripe weak or absent; large young have prominent dorsal and ventral spotting and yellow feet.
Dimorphism: Male has smoother skin; reduced dorsal blotching; nuptial pads (thickened skin) on forefeet during breeding season; throat pale as in female.
Similar species: *Bufo microscaphus californicus*: Has light colored stripe on head; very blunt snout; light-centered green, grey, brown or salmon color on dorsal side; lacks dorsal stripe; smaller total size.
Additional notes: A common species occupying a wide variety of habitats; frequently encountered during wet season on roads or near water at other times. When handled adults often vocalize (sounds like a peeping chick) while struggling.

Scientific name: *Bufo microscaphus californicus*
Four letter species code: BUMI
Size: 2-2.95 in (5.0-7.5 cm)
Common name: Arroyo Southwestern Toad
Distribution within study area: Los Angeles, Orange, Riverside, and San Diego Counties.

Distinguishing characters: A stocky, blunt-nosed, warty-skinned species; horizontal pupils; greenish, grey or salmon on dorsum with a light-colored stripe across head and eyelids; light sacral and mid-dorsal patches; large, oval, and widely-separated parotoid glands; weak or absent cranial crests.
Juveniles: Ashy-white, olive or salmon on dorsal side; with or without black spotting; red-tipped tubercles on back.
Dimorphism: None, unless in breeding season when males develop nuptial pads on forefeet.
Similar species: *Bufo boreas*: White or cream dorsal stripe on length of body; dark dorsal blotches containing skin glands; lacks blunt nose. *Bufo punctatus*: Flattened head with round parotoid glands the size of the eye.
Additional notes: Endangered and protected by federal law, any observations should be reported to U.S. Fish and Wildlife Service. Southern populations fragmented; uncommon within study area, although widespread. Prefers sandy or cobbly washes and associated upland habitats.

Scientific name: *Bufo punctatus* **Common name:** Red-Spotted Toad
Four letter species code: BUPU **Distribution within study area:** Riverside and San Diego Counties.
Size: 1.5-3 in (3.7-7.5 cm)
Distinguishing characters: A small toad species for this area; flattened head and body; light grey, olive or reddish brown dorsum with reddish or orange skin glands; whitish or buff venter with or without faint dark spotting; round parotoid glands; pointed snout; lacks cranial crests.
Juveniles: Similar to adults; more prominent ventral spotting; undersides of feet yellow.
Dimorphism: Male has dusky throat, and develops nuptial pads during breeding season.
Similar species: *Bufo boreas*: Has prominent mid-dorsal stripe; elongate parotoid glands; rounded snout and body; larger adult size.
Bufo microscaphus californicus: Lacks flattened, triangular head and round parotoid glands.
Additional notes: A species that occurs primarily along rocky streams and riverbeds, often in arid or semi-arid regions. Very localized on the coastal slope, but widespread on the deserts. May hybridize with *Bufo boreas* in Riverside Co., although this needs confirmation. Docile and easily handled with little or no skin gland secretions.

Scientific name: *Scaphiopus (Spea) hammondii* **Common name:** Western Spadefoot
Four letter species code: SCHA **Distribution within study area:** Entire study area.
Size: 1.5-2.95 in (3.8-7.5 cm)
Distinguishing characters: A relatively smooth-skinned species; eye is pale gold with vertical pupil; green or grey dorsum often with skin tubercles tipped in orange; whitish color on venter; wedge-shaped black spade on each hind foot.
Juveniles: Similar to adults, but spotting more distinct.
Dimorphism: None
Similar species: *Bufo boreas*: Has white dorsal stripe and pronounced parotoid glands. *Bufo microscaphus californicus*: Has very blunt snout and rough, warty skin. *Bufo punctatus*: Has flattened head and round parotoid glands. These species lack large spades on hind feet.
Additional notes: Populations are localized, but widespread. Prefers grassland, scrub and chaparral locally but could occur in oak woodlands. Nocturnal. Activity limited to wet season, summer storms, or during evenings with elevated substrate moisture levels. Easily handled, with less skin secretions than other toad species in study area. Their secretions smell like peanut butter and may cause sneezing. Genus may be changed to *Spea*, although currently not widely utilized.

Scientific name: *Hyla regilla*
Four letter species code: HYRE
Size: 1.0-2.0 in (2.5-5.0 cm)
Common name: Pacific Treefrog
Distribution within study area: Entire study area.

Distinguishing characters: A small species with a prominent dark brown or black eyestripe; variable dorsal coloration of shades of green, tan, reddish, grey, brown or black; dark triangular blotch on head; variable dark blotches or spotting depending on color phase, which can change dramatically from dark to light in a short time; venter whitish or cream with yellow on undersides of legs and lower abdomen; toe webbing reduced; small toe pads; smooth skin.
Juveniles: Similar to adults, although usually uniform in dorsal coloration.
Dimorphism: Male has yellow throat.
Similar species: *Hyla cadaverina*: Lacks eyestripe; has roughened-warty skin; larger toe webbing and pads.
Additional notes: Most common treefrog species in study area. Can occur distant from surface water in a variety of habitats.

Scientific name: *Hyla cadaverina*
Four letter species code: HYCA
Size: 1.14-2.0 in (2.9-5.0 cm)
Common name: California Treefrog
Distribution within study area: Creeks and rivers in all counties.

Distinguishing characters: A cryptically colored species, often resembling granitic stones; grey or light brown on dorsum with darker blotches; whitish venter; yellow on undersides of legs, groin and lower abdomen; conspicuous toe webbing and pads; dorsal skin roughened-warty.
Juveniles: Similar to adults.
Dimorphism: Male has dusky-yellow throat.
Similar species: *Hyla regilla*: Has prominent dark eyestripe; smoother skin; smaller toe webbing and pads.
Additional notes: A species most likely to occur along streams with abundant boulders and cobbles in channel. Distribution spotty and localized. Easily handled.

Scientific name: *Rana aurora draytonii*
Four letter species code: RAAU
Size: 1.75-5.51 in (4.4-14.0 cm)
Common name: California Red-Legged Frog
Distribution within study area: Sites supporting riparian habitats.

Distinguishing characters: A moderate to large species with dorsolateral folds; red lower abdomen and underside of hindlegs; brown, grey, olive or reddish color on dorsum with black flecks and dark, irregular, light-centered blotches; dark mask with whitish border above upper jaw; black and red or yellow mottling in groin; roughened skin on dorsum.
Juveniles: More pronounced dorsal spotting; may have yellow instead of red markings on underside of legs.
Dimorphism: Male has enlarged forelimbs, thumbs, and webbing.
Similar species: *Hyla regilla*, *Hyla cadaverina*: Both have toe pads. *Rana catesbeiana*: Lacks dorsolateral folds; has plain, unicolored dorsum; lacks red or yellow color in groin. *Rana boylii*: Lacks dorsolateral folds; has pale triangle on snout. *Rana muscosa*: Lacks dorsolateral folds; has yellow underside of legs; smoother skin; dark-tipped toes. *Rana pipiens*: Has more distinct dorsolateral folds; spotted with more uniform pattern; more pointed snout.
Additional notes: Uncommon or rare within study area. Report sightings immediately to U.S. Fish and Wildlife Service.

Scientific name: *Rana pipiens* complex
Four letter species code: RAPI
Size: 2-4.25 in (5-11.1 cm)
Common name: Leopard Frog
Distribution within study area: Sites supporting riparian habitats.
INTRODUCED: Native to majority of the U.S.

Distinguishing characters: A moderate species with well defined dorsolateral folds; white below; brown, grey, olive or green color on dorsum with oval or round dark spots; whitish border above upper jaw.
Juveniles: Less pronounced dorsal spotting.
Dimorphism: Male has enlarged thumbs during breeding season.
Similar species: *Hyla regilla*: Has toe pads. *Rana catesbeiana*: Lacks dorsolateral folds; has plain, unicolored dorsum. *Rana boylii*: Lacks dorsolateral folds; has pale triangle on snout. *Rana muscosa*: Lacks dorsolateral folds; has yellow underside of legs; smoother skin; dark-tipped toes. *Rana aurora*: Has less distinct dorsolateral folds; spotted with less uniform pattern; less pointed snout; red or yellow under hind legs.
Additional notes: Known from Santa Ana River (Prado Basin), uncommon or rare elsewhere in study area.

Scientific name: *Rana boylii*
Species code: RABO
Size: 1.5-2.8 in (3.7-7.1 cm)
Common name: Foothill Yellow-Legged frog
Distribution within study area: Los Angeles County.

Distinguishing characters: Small sized frog with dorsum grey, brown or reddish, commonly spotted or mottled but occasionally plainly colored; yellow under legs and may extend to abdomen; triangular, buff-colored patch on snout; no eye stripe; throat and chest often dark spotted; indistinct dorsolateral folds with granular skin.
Juveniles: Characteristic yellow on hind legs faint or absent.
Dimorphism: Male develops nuptial pads on thumb base during breeding season.
Similar species: *Hyla cadaverina*, *Hyla regilla*: Both have toe pads. *Rana catesbeiana*: Groin often dark spotted, lacking yellow color; smooth skin. *Rana muscosa*: Underside of hind legs and belly yellow to orange; dark colored lichenlike markings on dorsum. *Rana aurora*: Underside of hind legs and lower abdomen red overlying yellow ground color; prominent dorsolateral folds and eyestripe. *Rana pipiens*: Has distinct dorsolateral folds and uniform spots.
Additional notes: Uncommon or rare within study area, previously known only from a few river systems in Los Angeles County but could occur elsewhere.

Scientific name: *Rana muscosa*
Four letter species code: RAMU
Size: 2-3 in (5-7.5 cm)
Common name: Mountain Yellow-Legged Frog
Distribution within study area: Mountains in Los Angeles, Riverside, San Bernardino, and San Diego Counties.

Distinguishing characters: A small frog species; lower abdomen and underside of hindlegs yellow or orange; yellowish or reddish color on dorsum with black or brown spots or blotches; smells like garlic when handled.
Juveniles: Similar to adults, but less color under legs.
Dimorphism: Male develops nuptial pads on thumb base during breeding season.
Similar species: *Hyla cadaverina*, *Hyla regilla*: Both have toe pads. *Rana catesbeiana*: Groin often dark spotted, lacking yellow color; smooth skin. *Rana boylii*: Underside of hind legs yellow; triangular, buff-colored patch on snout. *Rana aurora*: Underside of hind legs and lower abdomen red overlying yellow ground color; prominent dorsolateral folds and eyestripe. *Rana pipiens*: Has distinct dorsolateral folds and uniform spots.
Additional notes: Uncommon or rare within study area; prefers mountain creeks and lakes.

Scientific name: *Rana catesbeiana*
Four letter species code: RACA
Size: 5.12-8.27 in (13.0-21.0 cm)
Common name: Bullfrog
Distribution within study area: Entire study area.
INTRODUCED: Occurs widespread in the Eastern U.S.
Distinguishing characters: Largest frog in California; prominent sacral humps; olive, green or brownish dorsum with vague spots or blotches; lighter green head; whitish, grey-mottled venter; legs blotched or banded; conspicuous eardrums; lacks dorsolateral folds.
Juveniles: Similar to adults, but more spotting and more grey on the dorsum.
Dimorphism: Male has yellow throat; eardrum larger than eye; swollen thumb base.
Similar species: *Rana aurora*: Has dorsolateral folds and reddish or yellow venter; dark mask bordered below in whitish. ***Rana pipiens*:** Has dorsolateral folds and dark spots on dorsum. ***Rana boylii*, *Rana muscosa*:** Both have either yellow or orange under legs and adults are only half the size of ***Rana catesbeiana***.
Additional notes: An introduced species; wary and difficult to capture. Male produces distinctive, deep-pitched vocalizations. Individuals will squawk when jumping into the water to excape. Usually found in association with permanent water, but can disperse over land at least several kilometers.

Scientific name: *Xenopus laevis*
Four letter species code: XELA
Size: 2-5.75 in (5-12.5 cm)
Common name: African Clawed Frog
Distribution within study area: Riparian habitats within entire study area.
INTRODUCED: Native to southern Africa.
Distinguishing characters: A highly aquatic species; smooth skin; forefeet unwebbed, hindfeet fully webbed with sharp black claws on inner toes; small head with blunt snout; eyes small, lidless and turned upward; olive to brown on dorsum with darker spots, blotches or mottling; whitish on venter; head and body flattened.
Juveniles: Similar to adults.
Dimorphism: Female is larger and has cloacal claspers.
Similar species: Should not be confused with other frog species. The only totally aquatic frog in California.
Additional notes: Introduced to the U.S. in the 1960's and feeds on native amphibian tadpoles. Will move overland at night during rains, and may show up in very unlikely places including golf course ponds, streams, ditches and lakes. Very slippery, but harmless, when handled, although has skin toxins.

Widespread tadpoles of coastal southern California

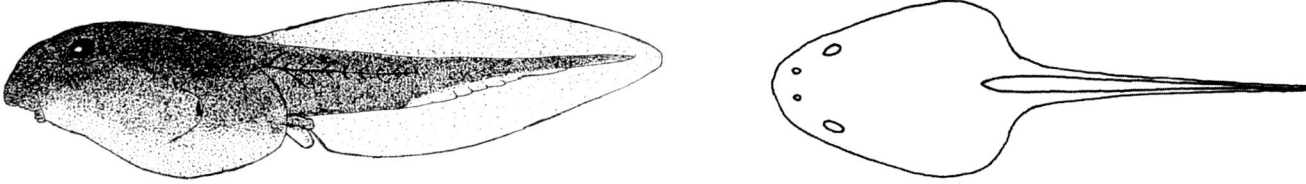

Western Toad (*Bufo boreas*), to approximately 45 mm., but usually smaller.

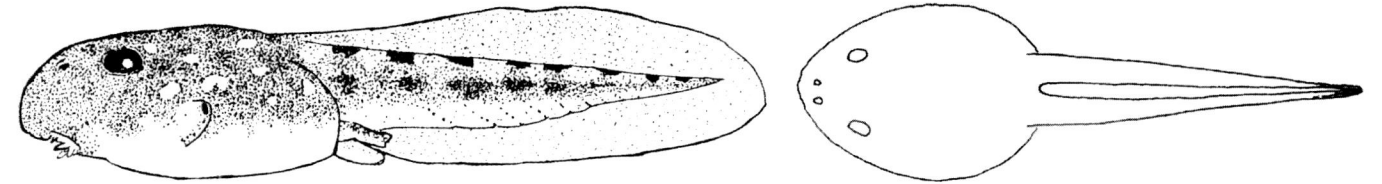

Arroyo Toad (*Bufo microscaphus californicus*), to approximately 35 mm., prefers flowing water.

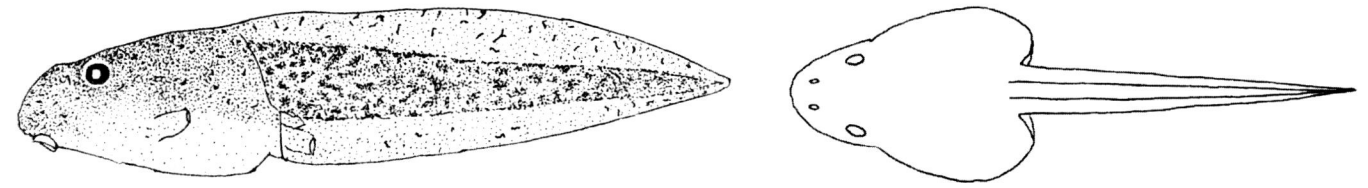

California Treefrog (*Hyla cadaverina*), to approximately 50 mm., usually in flowing creeks.

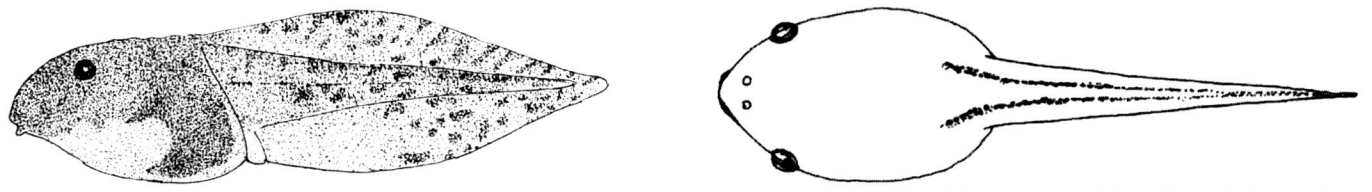

Pacific Treefrog (*Hyla regilla*), to approximately 45 mm., only species with eyes on side of head from above.

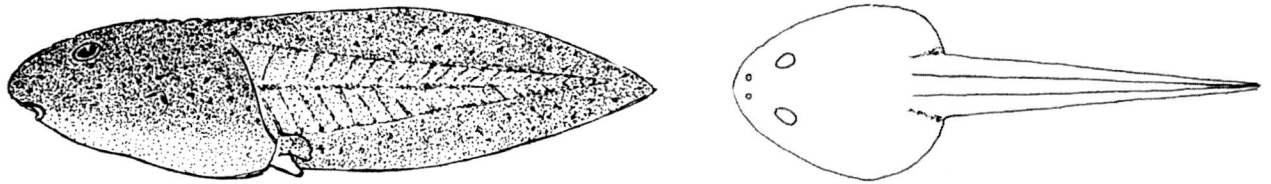

California Red-Legged Frog (*Rana aurora draytoni*), to approximately 75 mm., but may be larger.

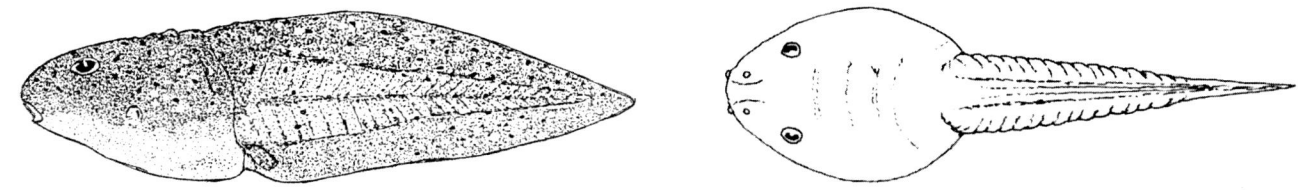

Bullfrog (*Rana catesbeiana*), to approximately 160 mm., the only tadpoles that overwinter.

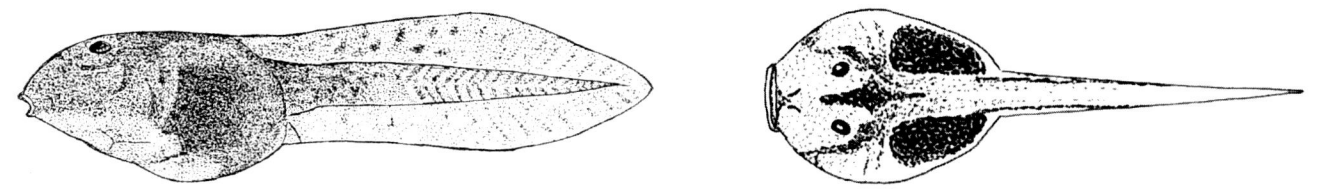

Western Spadefoot Toad (*Scaphiopus hammondii*), to approximately 60 mm., prefers standing pools.

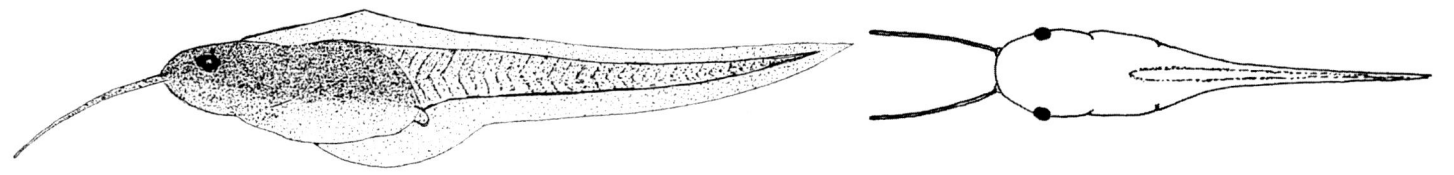

African Clawed Frog (*Xenopus laevis*), to approximately 50 mm., only tadpoles with tentacles.

Scientific name: *Clemmys marmorata*
Four letter species code: CLMA
Size: 4.7-7.2 in (12-18 cm)
Common name: Western Pond Turtle
Distribution within study area: All sites supporting riparian habitat.

Distinguishing characters: Low carapace with shields that have a network of lines or dashes of brown or black on a olive or dark background coming from its growth centers. Limbs and head olive, yellow, orange or brown often with darker lines, flecks or spots.
Juveniles: Tail as long as shell; head, limbs and tail marked with yellow; shields of the carapace have striking pattern of radiating lines.
Dimorphism: Male has a lighter throat; tail is much longer than that of female with cloaca extending past end of shell, whereas cloaca of female does not extend past end of shell; shell usually flatter and less marked than a female's, with underside concave.
Similar species: Although this is the only native turtle, *Trachemys scripta* is found introduced in many places but differs in having a greener shell, and large red markings on the side of the head.
Additional notes: An aquatic turtle that utilizes upland habitat seasonally. They occur in ponds, streams, lakes, ditches, and marshes.

Scientific name: *Trachemys scripta*
Four letter species code: TRSC
Size: 5.9-11.8 in (15-30 cm)
Common name: Slider/Red-eared Slider
Distribution within study area: Introduced generally in urban lakes and ponds.
INTRODUCED: Native to eastern U.S.

Distinguishing characters: Carapace has yellow streaking on olive or black shields; bright red, orange or yellow spot behind eyes; head and limbs are dark and striped with yellow; jagged rear edge of carapace.
Juveniles: Green coloration of carapace much brighter as juvenile. See upper right-hand picture.
Dimorphism: Male is usually darker and has longer nails on front feet than female.
Similar species: *Clemmys marmorata*: Has spotted head and limbs, and lacks red spot behind ear.
Additional notes: An aquatic turtle, although found sometimes moving overland to lay eggs or leaving a drying pond. Becoming increasingly more common in urban areas of southern California.

Scientific name: *Apalone spinifera*
Four letter species code: APSP
Size: 5-18 in (12-45 cm)
Common name: Spiny Softshell Turtle
Distribution within study area: Generally near lakes and rivers.
INTRODUCED: Native to central U.S.
Distinguishing characters: Extremely flattened turtle with leathery skin covering a soft, flexible shell; fleshy lips and flexible proboscis; limbs are under shell and toes are very webbed; looks like a pancake with legs.
Juveniles: Shell with black spots; dark mottling on head.
Dimorphism: Male has thick tail extending beyond carapace; female is blotched and mottled.
Similar species: None, as no other turtle in California is flattened in this way, or has a leathery shell.
Additional notes: Associated with permanent riparian systems, particularly artificial lakes in southern California; also in the Santa Ana River.

Scientific name: *Chelydra serpentina*
Four letter species code: CHSE
Size: 8-18.5 in (20-47 cm)
Common name: Snapping Turtle
Distribution within study area: Might show up in lakes or rivers.
INTRODUCED: Native to central and eastern U.S.
Distinguishing characters: Large headed turtle with hooked jaws; long crested tail; small narrow plastron, and a black, brown, or olive colored carapace.
Juveniles: Carapace with three lengthwise ridges; tail longer than shell; white spots around the shell margin.
Dimorphism: Male has a longer tail than female.
Similar species: All other California turtles have a larger plastron than ***Chelydra serpentina.***
Additional notes: Readily attempts to bite, handle with caution. Usually single large individuals are found associated with riparian habitat; no breeding populations are known in southern California.

Scientific name: *Anniella pulchra*
Four letter species code: ANPU
Size: 3.15-5.5 in (8.0-14.0 cm)
Common name: California Legless Lizard
Distribution within study area: Entire study area, except above 1,500 meters.
Distinguishing characters: Legless; silver or beige on dorsal side; greenish yellow venter; smooth shiny scales; black mid-dorsal line running length of body; additional lines where ventral and dorsal colors meet; distinct glossy black tip on tail, if not regenerated.
Juveniles: Cream or silver on dorsal half; grey or pale yellow on ventral half, but very similar to adults.
Dimorphism: None
Similar species: *Leptotyphlops humilis*: lacks dorsal stripes and eyelids.
Additional notes: Only legless lizard in California. A burrowing species seldom seen unless uncovered. Prefers loose soils associated with drainages and valley bottoms, but also occurs on hillsides. Can be nocturnal during summer, but rarely on roads at night.

Scientific name: *Elgaria multicarinatus*
Four letter species code: ELMU
Size: 3.1-7.25 in (7.8-18.4 cm)
Common name: Southern Alligator Lizard
Distribution within study area: Throughout study area.
Distinguishing characters: A long-bodied species with black and white crossbars on back and tail; brown, yellow, grey or reddish ground color; prominent fold along sides of body; dorsal scales strongly keeled; black or dusky bars on sides; yellow eyes; tail over twice the body length (if not regenerated); large head with pointed snout; small legs; broad, forked tongue; animals from mid-elevations in Orange County may be uniform grey with either red or black spots down back.
Juveniles: Broad dorsal stripe of yellow, tan, or reddish-gold; indistinct crossbands.
Dimorphism: Head broader and more triangular in adult males.
Similar species: *Eumeces gilberti*, *Eumeces skiltonianus*: Have smooth dorsal scales; lack lateral folds.
Additional notes: A distinctive species that can appear snake-like at first glance. Individuals will attempt to bite and defecate when handled; large adults can inflict painful bites, though not dangerous.

Scientific name: *Cnemidophorus hyperythrus*　　**Common name:** Orange-Throated Whiptail
Four letter species code: CNHY　　**Distribution within study area:** Orange, Riverside, and San Diego Counties.
Size: 2-2.83 in (5.0-7.2 cm)
Distinguishing characters: A distinctive species with five or six light colored stripes down a black, brown, or grey dorsal side; middle stripe may be forked at both ends; whitish-yellow or cream on venter; orange throat (females and juveniles may lack this character); head is yellow-brown to olive colored; tongue is forked and flicked continually.
Juveniles: Legs and tail are cobalt blue.
Dimorphism: Entire ventral surface of males including tail may be orange, although gravid females may also have some orange especially lining the lower jaw; colors are most distinct in breeding season; males have larger femoral pores than females.
Similar species: *Cnemidophorus tigris*: Has a spotted pattern (although juveniles of *Cnemidophorus tigris* from Orange and Riverside Counties can look very similar to *Cnemidophorus hyperythrus*); has larger head; lacks blue on legs present in juvenile *Cnemidophorus hyperythrus*; lacks orange underside. **Baja California Whiptail (*Cnemidophorus labialis*):** Although not recorded from the U.S. it occurs just south of the border on the coast and looks very similar to *Cnemidophorus hyperythrus* but differs in having 6-8 dorsal stripes and blue on legs in adult males, also lacks the orange underside of *Cnemidophorus hyperythrus*. *Eumeces skiltonianus*: Has very shiny scales; thicker tail; smaller legs.
Additional notes: A species with a distinctive, jerking gait.

Scientific name: *Cnemidophorus tigris multiscutatus*　　**Common name:** Coastal Western Whiptail
Four letter species code: CNTI　　**Distribution within study area:** Entire study area.
Size: 2.4-4.6 in (6.0-11.7 cm)
Distinguishing characters: A species with eight light-colored stripes that are often very indistinct, with crossbars in adults suggesting checkered appearance; dark markings on dorsum with yellow, tan or brown background; throat pale with black spots; long tail; enlarged, square scales on venter; dorsal scales fine and granular; tongue is forked and flicked continually.
Juveniles: Similar to adults, with distal portion of tail bright blue-green; in Orange and Riverside Counties they are striped.
Dimorphism: Enlarged femoral pores in males.
Similar species: *Cnemidophorus hyperythrus*: Striping more distinct; does not appear checkered or spotted; legs and tail cobalt blue in juveniles.
Additional notes: A distinctive species with a jerking gait, rarely sits still. Adults are surprisingly strong when handled and have very sharp claws.

Scientific name: *Eumeces skiltonianus*
Four letter species code: EUSK
Size: 1.73-2.95 in (4.4-7.5 cm)
Common name: Western Skink
Distribution within study area: Entire study area.

Distinguishing characters: Broad, brown stripe down middle of the back edged with black; pale whitish or golden stripes down sides, separated by a beige stripe beginning behind eyes; ventral side is whitish or grey; smooth scales; small legs; stripes appear faded in older adults.
Juveniles: Stripes are more contrasting; a bright cobalt blue tail.
Dimorphism: Male has orange to pinkish margin of lower jaw and ventral side of tail during breeding season. Sex of non-breeding adults and juveniles is difficult to distinguish.
Similar species: *Eumeces gilberti*: Dorsal stripe is black, edged with white, grey or olive striping; juveniles have waxy reddish or pink tail, adults are unicolor green-olive. *Cnemidophorus hyperythrus*: Has large, square ventral scales, forked tongue, larger legs, granular dorsal scales. *Elgaria multicarinatus*: Has keeled dorsal scales; prominent lateral fold.
Additional notes: A common species, although seldom seen in the open. Small, delicate species with smooth scales making individuals difficult to handle. Will lose tail easily, and body scales may come off of young individuals if handled too roughly. Lives in most terrestrial habitat types.

Scientific name: *Eumeces gilberti rubricaudatus*
Four letter species code: EUGI
Size: 2.7-4.6 in (6.8-11.7 cm)
Common name: Gilbert Skink or Western Red-Tailed Skink
Distribution within study area: Inland areas of all Counties.

Distinguishing characters: Adults uniform green, grey, olive or brown background; smooth scales; small legs; heavy bodied.
Juveniles: Light stripes on sides and dorsum enclosing a broad black or brown stripe; dark stripe stops near base of waxy-pink tail; stripes fade with growth and maturation.
Dimorphism: Male has broader head with orange or red temporal area and lower jaw.
Similar species: *Eumeces skiltonianus*: Striping prominent on lateral portions of tail; young with blue tails. *Elgaria multicarinatus*: Has keeled dorsal scales and prominent lateral fold; dorsal pattern with crossbars. *Cnemidophorus tigris*: Lacks smooth scales and has striking dorsal pattern of yellow crossbars on black background.
Additional notes: A large, robust skink seldom seen in the open. Adult individuals are surprisingly strong when handled. Juveniles are fragile, and should be handled with care.

Scientific name: *Coleonyx variegatus abbotti*　　**Common name:** Coastal Banded Gecko
Four letter species code: COVA　　**Distribution within study area:** Inland Orange, Riverside, San Bernardino and
Size: 1.65-2.91 in (4.2-7.4 cm)　　San Diego Counties.
Distinguishing characters: Soft skin; vertical pupils; movable eyelids; tail constricted at base and conspicuously banded; slender toes; dark body bands uniform in color and the same width as the yellow-pink background color; head uniformly purple, with thin yellow band over the collar; adults tend to retain juvenile color pattern in this subspecies, although body banding can diffuse with age.
Juveniles: Distal portion of tail bright yellow-green in hatchlings, but fades with age.
Dimorphism: Male has a prominent pelvic spur on each side of tail base, and have a few preanal pores.
Similar species: *Phyllodactylus xanti*: Lacks eyelids; has flattened toe pads; flatter body shape.
Additional notes: Nocturnal habits; often emits faint squeaks when handled. Very fragile species, handle with care. Some individuals from Riverside and San Bernardino Counties may have spots on their head and their dorsal bands may be more spotted and wider, characteristic of the Desert Banded Gecko (*Coleonyx variegatus variegatus*). The Barefoot Gecko (*Coleonyx switaki*) is a rock dwelling desert species that may conceivably be found on the coastal slope west of Jucumba or near Anza, but can be distinguished by having small tubercles on its dorsum.

Scientific name: *Phyllodactylus xanti*　　**Common name:** Leaf-Toed Gecko
Four letter species code: PHXA　　**Distribution within study area:** Possibly on coastal slopes in inland Riverside
Size: 1-2.5 in (2.5-6.2 cm)　　and San Diego Counties.
Distinguishing characters: A gecko with vertical pupils, immovable eyelids; leaf-like toe pads; dorsal granular scales interspersed with tubercles; brownish, grey or pinkish dorsum with a light venter; very fragile tail; often squeaks when handled.
Juveniles: Similar to adults.
Dimorphism: Male has preanal pores.
Similar species: *Xantusia henshawi*: Has large dark spots and no enlarged toe pads; lacks granular scales on dorsum.
Additional notes: Tail readily lost, be very careful handling this species.

Scientific name: *Xantusia henshawi*
Four letter species code: XAHE
Size: 1.4-2.75 in (3.6-7.0 cm)
Common name: Granite Night Lizard
Distribution within study area: Riverside and San Diego Counties.

Distinguishing characters: A flat-bodied species with a broad, flat head; soft skin; rounded, dark dorsal spots on pale yellow or cream background; scales granular on dorsum; large and squarish on ventral surface; large eyes with vertical pupils; lacks eyelids.
Juveniles: Similar to adults.
Dimorphism: Male has femoral pores.
Similar species: *Xantusia vigilis*: Has very small black dorsal spots; body and head not flattened; fewer rows of ventral scales.
Phyllodactylus xanti: Has enlarged toe pads and lacks large dark spots.
Additional notes: Most often occurs on rocky slopes with large, exfoliating boulders and abundant crevices, but is occasionally found in coastal sage scrub and chaparral without boulders. Active in crevices during the day, but moves on the surface at night.

Scientific name: *Xantusia vigilis*
Four letter species code: XAVI
Size: 1.0-1.77 in (2.6-4.5 cm)
Common name: Desert Night Lizard
Distribution within study area: Coastal slopes of mountains in Los Angeles County.

Distinguishing characters: A slim species; grey, olive, or dark brown dorsum with fine black speckles; beige stripe edged in black from eye to shoulder; smooth, granular scales on dorsum, large and squarish on venter; lacks eyelids; pupils vertical.
Juveniles: Similar to adults; darker dorsal coloration.
Dimorphism: Male has enlarged femoral pores.
Similar species: *Xantusia henshawi*: Has flattened head and body; prominent, large dorsal blotches; larger adult size.
Additional notes: May occur sparingly in study area. Often associated with dead branches of *Yucca*.

Scientific name: *Crotaphytus bicinctores*
Four letter species code: CRBI
Size: 2.75-4.57 in (6.9-11.6 cm)
Common name: Great Basin Collard Lizard
Distribution within study area: Washes in Los Angeles and San Bernardino Counties.
Distinguishing characters: A large-bodied species with a broad head, short snout, granular scales, and two distinct black collar markings; collar markings separated at dorsal midline by no more than 12 pale scales; tan to olive colored; light lines and spots and yellowish to orangish crossbands on body.
Juveniles: Similar to adults, more distinct banding.
Dimorphism: Male has enlarged postanal scales, blue-grey throat and large dark blotches on flanks.
Similar species: *Crotaphytus vestigium*: Black collars separated by more than 12 light scales. *Gambelia copei, Gambelia wislizenii*: Lack black collars.
Additional notes: Very uncommon. Powerful runner; bipedal. Adults can inflict painful bite. Prefers rocky areas, particularly washes.

Scientific name: *Crotaphytus vestigium*
Four letter species code: CRVE
Size: 2.75-4.5 in (6.9-11.2 cm)
Common name: Baja California Collared Lizard
Distribution within study area: Riverside and Eastern San Diego Counties.
Distinguishing characters: A large-bodied species with a broad head, short snout, granular scales, and two distinct black collar markings. Collar markings separated at dorsal midline by more than 12 pale scales. Tan to olive colored with broad dark crossbands on body.
Juveniles: Similar to adults, more distinct banding.
Dimorphism: Male has enlarged postanal scales, blue-grey throat and large dark blotches on flanks.
Similar species: *Crotaphytus bicinctores*: Black collars separated by 12 or less light scales. *Gambelia copei, Gambelia wislizenii*: Lack black collar.
Additional notes: Uncommon. Powerful runner; bipedal. Adults can inflict painful bite. Prefers rocky areas, especially washes.

Scientific name: *Gambelia copei*
Four letter species code: GACO
Size: 3.25-5.6 in (8-14 cm)
Common name: Baja California Leopard Lizard
Distribution within study area: Southern San Diego County (border area).

Distinguishing characters: Large, robust species with smoky grey background and darker grey or black dorsal spots, edged in lighter shade; dorsal pattern appears mottled or occelated; light crossbars on dorsum; light grey or white venter; small granular scales; large head distinct from neck, lining of mouth and throat purplish-black.
Juveniles: Similar to adults, more distinct banding across dorsum.
Dimorphism: Female develops red-orange blotches on ventral side during breeding season. Male has femoral pores.
Similar species: *Gambelia wislizenii*: Much lighter background coloration; north from northern San Diego County. *Sceloporus occidentalis*, *Sceloporus orcutti*: Have large keeled, pointed dorsal scales. *Uta stansburiana*: Has bluish-black blotches on sides of chest; lacks occelated dorsal pattern, much smaller.
Additional notes: Uncommon. Powerful runner; bipedal. Adults can inflict painful bite. Prefers chaparral habitats with open understory.

Scientific name: *Gambelia wislizenii*
Four letter species code: GAWI
Size: 3.25-5.75 in (8.1-14.4 cm)
Common name: Long-Nosed Leopard Lizard
Distribution within study area: Riverside and northeastern San Diego Counties.

Distinguishing characters: A large, robust species; round body and large, distinct head with long snout; dark spots on light dorsum with small, granular scales; appears mottled or occelated; ground color can be grey, pinkish or yellowish-brown; throat streaked with grey, lining of mouth and throat purplish-black.
Juveniles: Crossbars and spots more distinct; dorsum often rust colored.
Dimorphism: Males usually smaller than females, with femoral pores; females become reddish on sides, tail, and neck during breeding season.
Similar species: *Gambelia copei*: Has darker overall coloration (occurs in border area only of southern San Diego County). *Sceloporus occidentalis*, *Sceloporus orcutti*: Have keeled, pointed dorsal scales. *Uta stansburiana*: Smaller size and lacks occelated dorsal color pattern.
Additional notes: Uncommon. A powerful runner; bipedal. Very alert and wary, and hence it is extremely difficult to approach or capture. Adults can inflict painful bite and therefore must be handled with caution. Prefers open scrub and chaparral habitats.

Scientific name: *Phrynosoma coronatum*   **Common name:** Coast Horned Lizard
Four letter species code: PHCO   **Distribution within study area:** Entire study area.
Size: 2.3-4.2 in (5.9-10.6 cm)
Distinguishing characters: A distinctive flat-bodied species; two horns at back of head longer than surrounding spines; two rows of fringed scales down sides; two rows of enlarged pointed scales on margin of lower jaw; yellowish, brown or grey dorsum with contrasting wavy blotches of darker color; pointed scales on dorsum of body; beige or yellow venter with black spotting.
Juveniles: Similar to adults; cranial spines shorter and less pronounced.
Dimorphism: Male has broader tail at base, enlarged postanal scales, and femoral pores; adult females are larger than adult males.
Similar species: *Phrynosoma platyrhinos*: Has blunter snout; single row of spines on sides of body and lower jaw. Historically occurred along San Jacinto River wash on coastal slope, but it is not known if this population still exists.
Additional notes: Individuals may eject blood from eyes when handled. A gentle species that is easily handled, although may try to push cranial spines into hands while held.

Scientific name: *Phrynosoma platyrhinos*   **Common name:** Desert Horned Lizard
Four letter species code: PHPL   **Distribution within study area:** Riverside County (San Jacinto River wash).
Size: 2.5-3.75 in (6.4-9.4 cm)
Distinguishing characters: A distinctive flat-bodied species; one row of fringed scales down sides; one row of slightly enlarged scales on each side of the throat; beige, tan or reddish dorsum with contrasting, wavy blotches of darker color; pointed scales on dorsum of body; two large dark blotches on neck.
Juveniles: Similar to adults; cranial spines shorter and less pronounced.
Dimorphism: Male has broader tail at base and enlarged postanal scales; adult females are larger than adult males.
Similar species: *Phrynosoma coronatum*: Has less blunt snout; two rows of spines on sides of body and lower jaw.
Additional notes: Individuals may eject blood from eyes when handled. A gentle species that is easily handled.

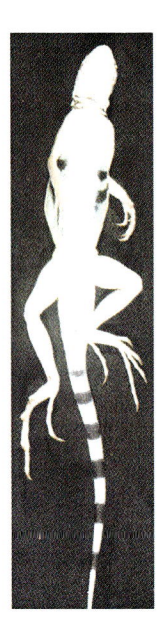

Scientific name: *Callisaurus draconoides*
Four letter species code: CADR
Size: 2.5-4 in (6.2-10 cm)
Common name: Zebra-Tailed Lizard
Distribution within study area: Riverside, San Bernardino, and northeast San Diego Counties.
Distinguishing characters: A long legged species with a flat tail; dark bands on underside of white tail and black belly markings at or anterior to midpoint of body; granular dorsal scales; gular fold; diagonal furrows separating upperlabials; grey dorsum with dusky markings, yellow on sides; light venter with pinkish or orange spot on throat.
Juveniles: Similar to adults.
Dimorphism: Male has enlarged postanal scales and more prominent belly markings.
Similar species: *Phrynosoma coronatum*: Only other lizard with flat tail, but has spines on head and body. *Uta stansburiana*: Lacks the dark bars under tail, and has blue-black side blotch.
Additional notes: Very uncommon in study area but common to east in the deserts; known only from washes. Quick runner, and will raise and wave tail when confronted and ready to escape.

Scientific name: *Petrosaurus mearnsi*
Four letter species code: PEME
Size: 2.5-3.5 in (6.2-8.7 cm)
Common name: Banded Rock Lizard
Distribution within study area: Riverside and southeastern San Diego Counties.
Distinguishing characters: An extremely flat bodied lizard with an olive, brown or grey dorsum and white or bluish spots on dorsum; single black collar, banded tail; granular scales on body with keeled tail and limb scales.
Juveniles: Similar to adults.
Dimorphism: Male has more pronounced throat pattern and brighter blue coloring; enlarged postanal scales.
Similar species: *Crotaphytus bicinctores*, *Crotaphytus vestigium*: Granular scales on tail, two dark collars; body shape not flattened.
Additional notes: Uncommon west of desert slope. Associated with boulder hillsides.

Scientific name: *Sceloporus occidentalis*
Four letter species code: SCOC
Size: 1.97-3.31 in (5.0-8.4 cm)
Common name: Western Fence Lizard
Distribution within study area: Entire study area.

Distinguishing characters: A robust species; dorsal scales keeled and pointed; dark brown or black blotched pattern; small blue spots on back and large one on throat; blue ventral patches, with a black mid-ventral stripe separating the patches; yellow or orange on rear under surfaces of limbs.
Juveniles: Lacks blue on throat; blue ventral patches faint or absent.
Dimorphism: Swollen tail base in males with paired enlarged scales just posterior of vent, and femoral pores; female has less vivid markings and lacks, or has smaller, pale blue ventral patches.
Similar species: *Sceloporus graciosus*: Occurs at high elevations often sympatric with *Sceloporus occidentalis*, but adults are smaller in size with distinct dorsal pattern of blotches and entire blue ventral patches in males; has white behind legs. *Sceloporus orcutti*: Usually occurs in association with rocks, has larger scales; can be green/purple on top and solid blue below; juveniles and females have black crossbars. *Uta stansburiana*: Has black to blue blotch behind forelimbs; smaller granular scales.
Additional notes: A common species occurring throughout study area.

Scientific name: *Sceloporus graciosus*
Four letter species code: SCGR
Size: 1.89-2.87 in (4.8-7.3 cm)
Common name: Southern Sagebrush Lizard
Distribution within study area: Above 1,500 meters in all counties except Orange.

Distinguishing characters: A small grey or brown species with contrasting blotches or crossbars on the dorsum; black bars on shoulder; rusty color in axilla, neck and sides of body; dorsal scales weakly keeled and pointed; blue ventral patches; white behind legs.
Juveniles: Similar to adults; but lacks blue throat and ventral patches, or are faintly present.
Dimorphism: Swollen tail base in males with enlarged paired scales just posterior of vent; femoral pores; blue-green flecks on dorsal scales; female has less vivid markings, and lacks or has pale, reduced blue ventral patches.
Similar species: *Sceloporus occidentalis*: Lacks rusty color on body; larger size, with scales keeled; has yellow-orange on ventral surfaces of legs. *Uta stansburiana*: Has bluish-black blotch behind forelimbs; lacks blue ventral patches and has granular dorsal scales.
Additional notes: Primarily a chaparral and montane species. Occurs sympatrically with *Uta stansburiana* and *Sceloporus occidentalis* at certain locations within study area at high elevations.

Scientific name: *Sceloporus orcutti*
Four letter species code: SCOR
Size: 3.00-4.25 in (7.6-10.8 cm)
Common name: Granite Spiny Lizard
Distribution within study area: Inland Orange, Riverside, and San Diego Counties.
Distinguishing characters: A large, robust species; dorsal scales strongly keeled and pointed on body and tail; wide purple mid-dorsal stripe; yellow-green and blue centered scales on body (males); distinct yellow-tan transverse bands on body and tail (juveniles and females).
Juveniles: Head rusty; dark markings on shoulders; crossbands on body evident.
Dimorphism: As described in distinguishing characters; additionally, male has deep blue ventral patches on chest and throat and femoral pores; female resembles juveniles in color and pattern.
Similar species: *Sceloporus occidentalis*: Smaller in size, with less pointed dorsal scales; lacks purple mid-dorsal stripe (males); lacks transverse banding (females and juveniles).
Additional notes: A colorful species that can be observed perched atop boulders from considerable distance. This species is primarily associated with rocky hillsides and outcrops.

Scientific name: *Sceloporus magister*
Four letter species code: SCMA
Size: 3.25-5.5 in (8.1-13.7 cm)
Common name: Desert Spiny Lizard
Distribution within study area: Sierra Pelona Mtns., northern Los Angeles County.
Distinguishing characters: A large, robust species; dorsal scales strongly keeled and pointed on body and tail; black partial collar behind neck; yellow to tan dorsal coloration.
Juveniles: Small blotches and crossbands on body evident.
Dimorphism: Male has deep blue ventral patches on chest and throat and has femoral pores; female head color is reddish when breeding.
Similar species: *Sceloporus occidentalis*: Smaller in size, with less pointed dorsal scales; lacks yellow or tan dorsal coloration; lacks black partial neck collar.
Additional notes: A desert species that barely makes it to the Pacific slope in Los Angeles County. Recently found along the lower Sweetwater River in San Diego County, although this population is probably introduced.

Scientific name: *Uta stansburiana*
Four letter species code: UTST
Size: 1.57-2.36 in (4.0-6.0 cm)
Common name: Side-Blotched Lizard
Distribution within study area: Entire study area.

Distinguishing characters: A small species; a conspicuous bluish-black blotch on each side behind the forelimbs; dorsum blotched or spotted with blue, orange, yellow, brown and/or black; whitish to grey on venter; orange or light blue patch on throat, and no blue belly patches.
Juveniles: Similar to adult female in pattern; lacks blue-black spots on sides.
Dimorphism: Male has swollen tail base, blue and yellow flecks on mid-dorsal side, and enlarged postanal scales; female lacks blue and yellow mid-dorsal flecks and is blotched dorsally in brown and black.
Similar species: ***Sceloporus graciosus, Sceloporus occidentalis*:** Have keeled, pointed dorsal scales; lack bluish-black spots on side behind forelimb.
Additional notes: A common species throughout the study area, but prefers open habitats with rocks. Occurs sympatrically with *Sceloporus occidentalis* at many study sites and with *Sceloporus graciosus* at some high elevation study sites.

Scientific name: *Urosaurus microscutatus*
Four letter species code: URMI
Size: 1.5-2 in (3.7-5 cm)
Common name: Small-Scaled Lizard
Distribution within study area: Southern San Diego County (border area).

Distinguishing characters: A small species; two rows of dark brown or black blotches on dorsum and a brown, grey, or sooty background color; dorsal scales granular; enlarged scales along midline of body; prominent gular fold on throat; loose folds along sides of body; long tail.
Juveniles: Similar to adults; pale yellow-orange throat patch.
Dimorphism: Male has orange-centered blue throat patch and blue patches on venter; paired, enlarged postanal scales; females smaller, lacking blue ventral patches and enlarged postanal scales.
Similar species: ***Sceloporus occidentalis, Sceloporus orcutti*:** Have keeled, pointed dorsal scales; lack gular fold. ***Uta stansburiana*:** Lacks blue ventral patches; has bluish-black spot on sides behind forelimbs.
Additional notes: Occurs in small, localized populations in extreme southern portion of study area only. Usually associated with rocky hillsides or dry riparian woodlands. Frequently perches on trees. Apparently, this species may be synonymous with *Urosaurus nigricaudus* from Baja California.

Scientific name: *Charina bottae umbratica*
Four letter species code: CHBO
Size: 11.8-17.3 in (30-44 cm)
Common name: Southern Rubber Boa
Distribution within study area: Above 2,000 meters in the San Jacinto and San Bernardino Mountains.

Distinguishing characters: A heavy-bodied snake with smooth, shiny scales that look and feel like rubber; small eyes with vertically oval pupils; large plate-like scales on top of head; olive-green, buff, or tan dorsum with contrasting yellowish or cream venter; subcaudal scales undivided; tail blunt, with shield-like scale at tip.
Juveniles: Generally lighter; pink or tan dorsum and light yellow to pink venter.
Dimorphism: Anal spurs well developed in the male, small or absent in the female.
Similar species: *Lichanura trivirgata*: Lacks enlarged scales on top of head and has enlarged chin scales; also has three dorsal stripes and mottled venter.
Additional notes: Often rolls body into ball concealing head when handled or injured. A secretive species that is seldom observed in the open. Generally associated with rocky outcrops in coniferous forests.

Scientific name: *Charina (Lichanura) trivirgata roseofusca*
Four letter species code: LITR
Size: 22.4-35.4 in (57-90 cm)
Common name: Coastal Rosy Boa
Distribution within study area: Entire study area, generally inland.

Distinguishing characters: Heavy-bodied species with smooth, shiny scales; small eyes with vertically oval pupils; chin shields enlarged; lacks plate-like scales on top of head; bluish-grey ground color with three broad brown, orange, or reddish brown longitudinal stripes; same color mottling on interspaces; cream venter, spotted with grey; some individuals lack contrast between stripe and ground color, appearing unicolored, either reddish or silvery grey; subcaudal scales undivided.
Juveniles: Lighter ground color; contrasting dorsal pattern more distinct.
Dimorphism: Anal spurs well developed in the male; weak or absent in the female.
Similar species: *Charina bottae*: Lacks dorsal striping; has plate-like scales on top of head; lacks enlarged chin shields; occurs only in San Jacinto and San Bernardino Mountains within study area.
Additional notes: A gentle species that is easily handled; often rolls body into ball concealing head when handled or injured. Appears to be declining on coast, where it was once common. Genus name for this species should now be *Charina*, although most people still use the name *Lichanura*.

Juvenile **AREL** above

Scientific name: *Arizona elegans occidentalis*
Four letter species code: AREL
Size: 25.2-38.9 in (64-99 cm)
Common name: California Glossy Snake
Distribution within study area: Historically below 1,500 meters in all counties.
Distinguishing characters: Smooth, glossy scales; chocolate colored body blotches on a tan or light brown ground color; prominent eye stripe; eyes with slightly vertical pupils; countersunk lower jaw; single anal scale.
Juveniles: Similar to adults, but blotches darker.
Dimorphism: None
Similar species: *Pituophis melanoleucus*: Has keeled scales; eyes with round pupils; divided anal scale. *Hypsiglena torquata*: Has a triangular flattened head; vertical pupils; white labial scales.
Additional notes: An uncommon species in focal area, although historically this subspecies was widespread. Primarily nocturnal, it is associated with loose soils in valleys and washes suitable for burrowing. Gentle, calm, and easily handled.

Scientific name: *Pituophis melanoleucus annectens*
Four letter species code: PIME
Size: 31.5-55.5 in (80-141 cm)
Common name: San Diego Gopher Snake
Distribution within study area: Entire study area.
Distinguishing characters: A large species; yellow or cream dorsum becoming orange-tinted toward tail; black or brown dorsal blotches on body; widely spaced on tail; smaller blotches on sides; venter yellow or yellow-orange, pinkish toward tail; faint mottling on venter especially tail; dark line across head between orbit of eyes; orange or brick colored eyes with round pupils; dorsal scales keeled.
Juveniles: Similar to adults.
Dimorphism: None
Similar species: *Arizona elegans*: Has smooth scales; countersunk lower jaw; single anal plate. *Coluber constrictor* (**juvenile**): Has smooth scales; large dark eyes. *Hypsiglena torquata*: Has flat head; white labial scales; vertical pupils.
Additional notes: A large species that may hiss loudly, vibrate tail, and strike when annoyed. Usually becomes calm when handled. Widespread in most habitat types.

Scientific name: *Diadophis punctatus* **Common name:** Western Ringneck Snake
Four letter species code: DIPU **Distribution within study area:** Entire study area.
Size: 10.4-16.1 in (26-41 cm)
Distinguishing characters: A small, slender species with an olive, brownish, blue-grey or green dorsum and a conspicuous yellow or orange neck band; venter yellow-orange, becoming coral toward tail with conspicuous black spots often forming rows; dark head.
Juveniles: Similar to adults, but with darker dorsal coloration.
Dimorphism: Male has tubercles on scales above vent.
Similar species: *Tantilla planiceps*: Has cream neck band; black head; lighter orange-tan dorsal coloration; lacks black spotting on coral-orange venter.
Additional notes: A gentle species that is easily handled; often coils tail into corkscrew shape displaying brilliant coral undersurface.

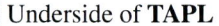

Scientific name: *Tantilla planiceps* **Common name:** California Black-Headed Snake
Four letter species code: TAPL **Distribution within study area:** Entire study area under 1,500 meters.
Size: 6.5-11.5 in (16-29 cm)
Distinguishing characters: A small, slender species; light brown, tan to olive-grey dorsum; narrow cream or white neck band; flattened black head; orange or coral-red venter edged with white.
Juveniles: Similar to adults.
Dimorphism: None
Similar species: *Diadophis punctatus*: Has darker dorsal coloration; orange or red neck band (may be broken or absent in some individuals); orange-yellow venter with black spotting, becoming coral to red on ventral surface of tail.
Additional notes: A small, secretive species that is seldom seen. Individuals are easily handled. Often occurs under rocks.

Scientific name: *Coluber constrictor mormon*
Four letter species code: COCO
Size: 14.2-29.5 in (36-75 cm)
Common name: Western Yellow-Bellied Racer
Distribution within study area: Entire study area, although rare in Riverside and southern San Diego Counties.
Distinguishing characters: A slender snake with large eyes and round pupils; smooth scales and brown, olive or bluish on dorsum; white or pale yellow venter; tail long and slender.
Juveniles: Lighter background with brown crossbars or conjoined blotches across back; smaller blotches on sides.
Dimorphism: None
Similar species: *Arizona elegans*: Has countersunk lower jaw. *Pituophis melanoleucus*: Has keeled scales. *Hypsiglena torquata*: Has flat head and vertical pupils. These species can resemble juveniles of *Coluber constrictor*. Adult *Coluber constrictor* are fairly distinctive, but could be confused with *Thamnophis hammondii* (has keeled dorsal scales and yellow side stripes).
Additional notes: A fast moving species that is difficult to capture in the wild. May excrete musk and bite when handled. Prefers grasslands and riparian habitats.

Scientific name: *Thamnophis hammondii*
Four letter species code: THHA
Size: 15.4-28.4 in (39-72 cm)
Common name: Two-Striped Garter Snake
Distribution within study area: Entire study region, generally associated with natural wetlands.
Distinguishing characters: A species that lacks a mid-dorsal stripe; olive, brown or brownish-grey dorsum; dull yellow, orange, or salmon venter; lengthwise rows of small, dark spots; yellow stripes on sides; throat pale; eyes brick color with round pupils; red tongue; dorsal scales keeled; usually black patches on neck behind head; occasional melanic individuals lacking side stripes.
Juveniles: Similar to adults.
Dimorphism: Female has extremely constricted tail immediately posterior of the base.
Similar species: *Thamnophis elegans*: Has a mid-dorsal stripe; lacks yellow lateral spotting. *Thamnophis sirtalis*: Has mid-dorsal stripe; red lateral blotches. *Masticophis lateralis*: Has smooth scales; black tongue. *Coluber constrictor*: Smooth scales and lacks side stripes.
Additional notes: Only garter snake species within study area that lacks mid-dorsal stripe. Excretes foul smelling musk when handled.

Scientific name: *Masticophis flagellum piceus*
Four letter species code: MAFL
Size: 24.4-54.3 in (62-138 cm)
Common name: Red Coachwhip or Red Racer
Distribution within study area: Entire area, except within 12 kilometers of the Mexican Border, and over 2,000 meters elevation.
Distinguishing characters: A species with highly variable dorsal coloration; tan, grey, red, or pink with bold black or brown crossbars or blotches on neck which may blend together; venter pink; slender body and tail; large eyes with round pupils; often described as a red snake with a black head.
Juveniles: Black, brown or tan transverse bands on lighter background; black neck markings absent in hatchlings and faint in juveniles less than 24 in (61 cm) in length.
Dimorphism: None
Similar species: *Masticophis lateralis*: Has distinct yellow lateral stripes. *Coluber constrictor*: Lacks dark crossbars or blotches on neck (adults); juveniles of *Coluber constrictor* appear more blotched than banded. *Masticophis flagellum fulginosus*: Only occurs in southern San Diego County (border area only); olive colored or jet black on dorsum.
Additional notes: A fast moving diurnal snake that is difficult to capture. Bites, excretes musk and twists body when handled. Large individuals should be handled with caution.

Scientific name: *Masticophis flagellum fulginosus*
Four letter species code: MAFU
Size: 24-52 in (62-132 cm)
Common name: Baja California Coachwhip
Distribution within study area: Southern San Diego County, only within 12 kilometers of the Mexican Border.
Distinguishing characters: A slender species; dark grey-brown or olive above with white spotting on sides, becoming more prominent on neck and upper body; dark blotches on neck and head; venter cream, and spotted with paired black spots toward head; slender body and tail; large eyes with round pupils; occasional inland individuals may be completely black on dorsum.
Juveniles: Black, brown, or tan transverse bands on lighter (grey) background; neck markings absent in hatchlings and faint in juveniles less than 24 in (61 cm) in length.
Dimorphism: None
Similar species: *Masticophis lateralis*: Has distinct yellow lateral stripes. *Coluber constrictor*: Lacks dark crossbars or blotches on neck (adults); juveniles of *Coluber constrictor* appear more blotched than banded. *Masticophis flagellum piceus*: Generally red body with black head and neck; pink venter.
Additional notes: A fast moving diurnal snake that is difficult to capture. Tends to be less aggressive than *Masticophis flagellum piceus*, and instead of striking it typically puts its body into a ball and flattens its head.

Scientific name: *Masticophis lateralis* **Common name:** California Whipsnake or Striped Racer
Four letter species code: MALA **Distribution within study area:** Entire study area.
Size: 22.4-49.2 in (57-125 cm)
Distinguishing characters: A slender species; black, or brownish on dorsum; lighter color toward tail; yellow or white dark-edged stripe down sides from back of head to vent; white, cream or pale yellow venter becoming salmon/pink at tail; large eyes with round pupils; smooth scales.
Juveniles: Similar to adults.
Dimorphism: None
Similar species: *Masticophis flagellum*: Lacks lateral striping. *Salvadora hexalepis*: Has enlarged thickened rostral scale and mid-dorsal stripe. *Thamnophis hammondii*: Has keeled scales and red tongue; olive on dorsum. *Thamnophis elegans*: Has keeled scales and red tongue; mid-dorsal stripe.
Additional notes: An alert, fast moving, diurnal snake that is difficult to capture. May bite and excrete musk when handled.

Scientific name: *Salvadora hexalepis virgultea* **Common name:** Coast Patch-Nosed Snake
Four letter species code: SAHE **Distribution within study area:** Entire study area.
Size: 22-34 in (56-87 cm)
Distinguishing characters: A slender species; yellow or beige mid-dorsal stripe bordered by dark tan or brown side stripes; dull white venter, becoming orangish toward tail; rostral scale large, thick and triangular in shape; large, dark eyes with round pupils; smooth scales; divided anal scale.
Juveniles: Similar to adults.
Dimorphism: Male has keeled scales above vent and at base of tail.
Similar species: *Lampropeltis getula* (striped phase): Lacks the distinctive enlarged rostral scale. *Thamnophis elegans*: Has keeled dorsal scales and red tongue; strong musk when handled.
Additional notes: An alert fast-moving diurnal species that is difficult to capture. Individuals are typically gentle when handled.

Scientific name: *Lampropeltis getula californiae* **Common name:** California Kingsnake
Four letter species code: LAGE **Distribution within study area:** Entire study area.
Size: 19.7-43.8 in (50-111 cm)
Distinguishing characters: A polymorphic species with various color and pattern phases consisting primarily of alternating bands of black or brown, and white or yellow (banded phase) or longitudinal stripes of these same colors (striped phase); some individuals exhibit partial patterns of both and can appear marbled, spotted, or blotched; scales smooth and glossy; snout light colored; single anal scale.
Juveniles: Similar to adults.
Dimorphism: None
Similar species: *Lampropeltis zonata*: Has first white band crossing temporal area of head, usually with some red banding on body either anteriorally, or within the black bands; lacks light color on snout. ***Salvadora hexalepis*:** Has distinct triangular thickened rostral scale and large eyes, but similar dorsal pattern to striped phase of ***Lampropeltis getula***. ***Thamnophis elegans*:** Has similar pattern to striped phase but has keeled dorsal scales.
Additional notes: Individuals may excrete musk, vibrate tail, and bite when handled. Widespread in many habitats.

Scientific name: *Rhinocheilus lecontei* **Common name:** Western Long-Nosed Snake
Four letter species code: RHLE **Distribution within study area:** Generally below 1,500 meters elevation.
Size: 18.9-29.5 in (48-75 cm)
Distinguishing sharacters: A slender species; cream ground color; black dorsal saddles with red interspaces; cream or yellow venter; black spotting on a white head; black saddles speckled with white on the sides; very pointed snout; countersunk lower jaw; anterior portion of subcaudal scales undivided in most individuals.
Juveniles: Banding more pronounced; speckling on sides faint or absent.
Dimorphism: None
Similar species: *Lampropeltis getula*, *Lampropeltis zonata*: Have banding completely around body; all subcaudals divided; rounded snouts; lack countersunk lower jaw.
Additional notes: A gentle species that vibrates tail when annoyed. Some individuals may hemorrhage from the cloaca and excrete musk when handled.

Scientific name: *Lampropeltis zonata pulchra* **Common name:** San Diego Mountain Kingsnake
Four letter species code: LAZO **Distribution within study area:** Creek drainages, and above 500 meters in Los Angeles, Orange, Riverside, and San Diego Counties.
Size: 20-40 in (51-102 cm)
Distinguishing characters: A colorful species with black, white and red crossbands encircling body and tail; smooth, glistening scales; snout and eyes generally black; southern populations often with red spotting on top of head; usually 37 or fewer sets of bands (triads), and most red bands connect across the dorsum.
Juveniles: Similar to adults.
Dimorphism: None
Similar species: ***Lampropeltis getula***: Has light color on snout and no red markings. ***Rhinocheilus lecontei***: Has body bands that do not encircle body, but form saddles; pointed snout, with countersunk lower jaw; undivided subcaudal scales on anterior portion of tail.
Additional notes: A montane species that can occur at lower elevations along wooded drainages in mountains. The same species code is used for both subspecies as they are allopatric on mountains. This species is **NOT** poisonous.

Scientific name: *Lampropeltis zonata parvirubra* **Common name:** San Bernardino Mountain Kingsnake
Four letter species code: LAZO **Distribution within study area:** Above 1,500 meters elevation in Los Angeles, Riverside, and San Bernardino Counties.
Size: 20-40 in (51-102 cm)
Distinguishing characters: A colorful species with black, white and red crossbands encircling body and tail; smooth, glistening scales; snout and eyes generally black; may have red spotting on top of head; usually 37 or more sets of bands (triads), and many red bands do not connect across the dorsum.
Juveniles: Similar to adults.
Dimorphism: None
Similar species: ***Lampropeltis getula***: Has light color on snout and no red markings. ***Rhinocheilus lecontei***: Has body bands that do not encircle body, but form saddles; pointed snout, with countersunk lower jaw; undivided subcaudal scales on anterior portion of tail.
Additional notes: A montane species that can occur in talus slopes in mountains. This species is NOT poisonous.

Scientific name: *Thamnophis elegans elegans*
Four letter species code: THEL
Size: 15-24 in (39-61 cm)
Common name: Mountain Garter Snake
Distribution within study area: Above 1,500 meters in the San Bernardino Mountains.

Distinguishing characters: A slender species; black or dark grey-brown dorsum; yellow, orange, or white mid-dorsal and side stripes; pale yellowish or white venter; dorsal scales keeled; red tongue.
Juveniles: Similar to adults.
Dimorphism: Female has extemely constricted tail immediately posterior to vent.
Similar species: *Thamnophis hammondii*: Lacks mid-dorsal stripe. *Thamnophis sirtalis*: Has red lateral blotches; does not occur above 1,000 meters in our area. *Salvadora hexalepis*: Has enlarged thickened triangular rostral scale and black tongue. *Lampropeltis getula* (**striped**): Lacks keeled scales and red tongue.
Additional notes: A montane species. Some individuals lack continous mid-dorsal stripe which can be limited to nape only. Excretes foul smelling musk when handled.

Scientific name: *Thamnophis sirtalis infernalis*
Four letter species code: THSI
Size: 15-30 in (38-77 cm)
Common name: California Red-Sided Garter Snake
Distribution within study area: Below 1,000 meters from Los Angeles County south through central San Diego County.

Distinguishing characters: A slender species; dark olive to nearly black ground color with red blotches; head olive; yellow mid-dorsal and lateral stripes well defined; yellow-green or blue venter; eyes well defined; dorsal scales keeled; red tongue.
Juveniles: Similar to adults.
Dimorphism: Female has extremely constricted tail immediately posterior to vent.
Similar species: *Thamnophis hammondii*: Lacks mid-dorsal stripe; no red markings on sides. *Thamnophis elegans*: Has mid-dorsal stripe and solid dark sides; lacks red blotches; only occurs in the San Bernardino Mountains.
Additional notes: A rare snake within study area, but apparently associated with extensive riparian systems. Excretes foul smelling musk when handled.

Scientific name: *Hypsiglena torquata*
Four letter species code: HYTO
Size: 9.8-13.8 in (25-35 cm)
Common name: Night Snake
Distribution within study area: Entire study area.

Distinguishing characters: A pale grey, beige or light brown species; brown paired blotches on dorsum; usually three large black blotches on the neck, sometimes merging; venter whitish or yellow; flat head; vertical pupils; brown bar behind eyes; white labial scales; scales smooth, often with irridescence.
Juveniles: Similar to adults.
Dimorphism: None
Similar species: *Trimorphodon biscutatus*: Has V-shaped marking on head; pale crossbars; hexagonal markings on body; larger eyes and scales. *Arizona elegans*, *Coluber constrictor* (**juvenile**): Have round pupils. *Pituophis melanoleucus*: Has round pupils; keeled scales. *Crotalus viridis*: Has rattle on tail.
Additional notes: May flatten head, coil tightly, and vibrate tail when disturbed. A gentle species that is easily handled. Often found under rocks.

Scientific name: *Trimorphodon biscutatus vandenburghi*
Four letter species code: TRBI
Size: 17.7-35.4 in (45-90 cm)
Common name: California Lyre Snake
Distribution within study area: Generally below 1,500 meters in elevation throughout area.

Distinguishing characters: A slender species with a laterally flattened body; broad head, slender neck; V-shaped marking on top of head resembling lyre; light brown or grey on dorsal side with brown blotches; blotches roughly hexagonal and bisected with a pale crossbar; cream or white venter with pale brown spots; smooth scales; large, protruding eyes with vertical pupils.
Juveniles: Similar to adults in pattern, but highly contrasting in dorsal color; hatchlings can appear nearly black and white.
Dimorphism: Female is larger than male with extremely constricted tail; male's tail thickened midway between anal scale and tip, and is longer than that of a female's.
Similar species: *Hypsiglena torquata*: Has dark blotches on neck; dark bar across head; head less distinct from neck; lacks V-shaped markings on top of head. *Arizona elegans*, *Pituophis melanoleucus*: Have round pupils.
Additional notes: A nervous species that hisses and vibrates rattleless tail when annoyed. Nocturnal and secretive, in our area it is usually associated with rocky hillsides and outcrops.

Scientific name: *Crotalus ruber (exsul)*
Four letter species code: CRRU
Size: 29-63 in (73-160 cm)
Common name: Red Diamond Rattlesnake
Distribution within study area: Orange, Riverside, and San Diego Counties.

Distinguishing characters: A rattlesnake with tan, pink, or reddish dorsal color and prominent light-edged diamonds of darker hue; faint pepper marks over dorsal pattern; tail with conspicuous black and white rings; broad vertical eye stripe edged in lighter color.
Juveniles: Dark and light grey hues in pattern, changing to reddish with age.
Dimorphism: Male tail is more stout.
Similar species: *Crotalus mitchellii*: Has diffused pattern; fine salt-and-pepper speckled appearance; lacks eye stripe. *Crotalus viridis*: Lacks conspicuous black and white tail bands; juveniles have yellow-green tail.
Additional notes: A large species often associated with coastal sage scrub, rocky hillsides, and outcrops. Relatively docile, although some individuals may hiss loudly and/or rattle when annoyed. **VENOMOUS**; don't handle or use extreme caution. The name for this species may be changed to *exsul* in the future.

Scientific name: *Crotalus viridis helleri*
Four letter species code: CRVI
Size: 22-40 in (55-102 cm)
Common name: Southern Pacific Rattlesnake
Distribution within study area: Entire study area.

Distinguishing characters: A rattlesnake with grey, olive, or brown ground color and light-edged, darker diamonds on dorsum; blotches on sides dark, angular and also light-edged; light stripe from corner of mouth to eye; low-contrast dark tail rings, with terminal ring poorly defined and twice as wide; venter light yellow or cream with faint blotching; high elevation populations can be very dark or black dorsally, with little or no pattern definition.
Juveniles: Similar to adults, but with bright yellow-green tail.
Dimorphism: Male has a more stout tail than the female.
Similar species: *Crotalus ruber*: Has conspicuous black and white banded tail; usually tannish or reddish dorsal coloration. *Crotalus mitchellii*: Has black and white bands on tail; highly diffused dorsal pattern; lacks eye stripe.
Additional notes: A nervous species that will aggressively defend itself when annoyed. **VENOMOUS**; don't handle or use extreme caution. Occurs in all habitat types in the focal area.

Scientific name: *Leptotyphlops humilis*
Four letter species code: LEHU
Size: 7.2-13.0 in (18-33 cm)
Common name: Western Blind Snake
Distribution within study area: Entire study area.

Distinguishing characters: A thin cylindrical species with no neck constriction; blunt head and tail; purplish, brown or pink dorsum with silvery sheen; light venter; no enlarged ventral scutes; eyes vestigial, appearing as dark spot beneath head scales; spinelike terminal scale on tail tip.
Juveniles: Similar to adults, except lighter in color.
Dimorphism: None
Similar species: *Anniella pulchra*: Has eyelids; black dorsal striping and black tail tip.
Additional notes: Difficult to hold since they will squeeze out of hands. Excretes watery fluid that has a musky odor.

Scientific name: *Crotalus mitchellii pyrrhus*
Four letter species code: CRMI
Size: 21.6-39.4 in (55-100 cm)
Common name: Southwestern Speckled Rattlesnake
Distribution within study area: Orange, Riverside, San Bernardino, and San Diego Counties.

Distinguishing characters: A rattlesnake with highly variable dorsal coloration- white to dark grey or shades of pink or orange; dark, diffused bands on back often split by lighter color; keeled scales; large head; salt-and-pepper speckles over entire dorsal pattern; tail with black and white bands, often incompletely encircling tail.
Juveniles: Similar to adults.
Dimorphism: None
Similar species: *Crotalus ruber*: Has distinct diamond pattern on dorsum; black and white tail bands completely encircle tail.
Crotalus viridis: Has diamond pattern on dorsum; prominent eye stripe; lacks black and white tail bands.
Additional notes: An alert, nervous species most often associated with rocky hillsides and outcrops. **VENOMOUS**; don't handle or use extreme caution.

Salamanders

Toads and Frogs

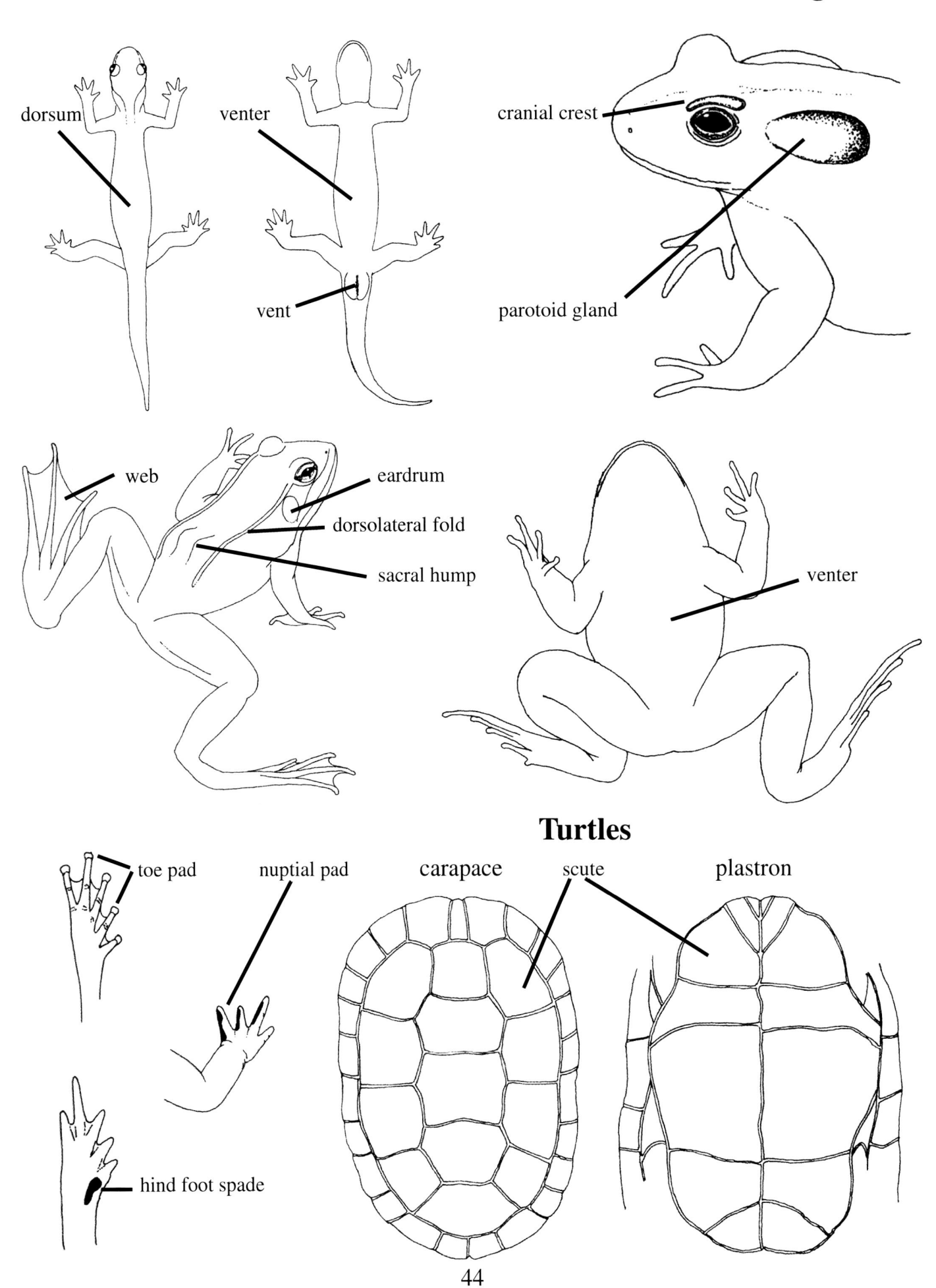

Turtles

Lizards and Snakes

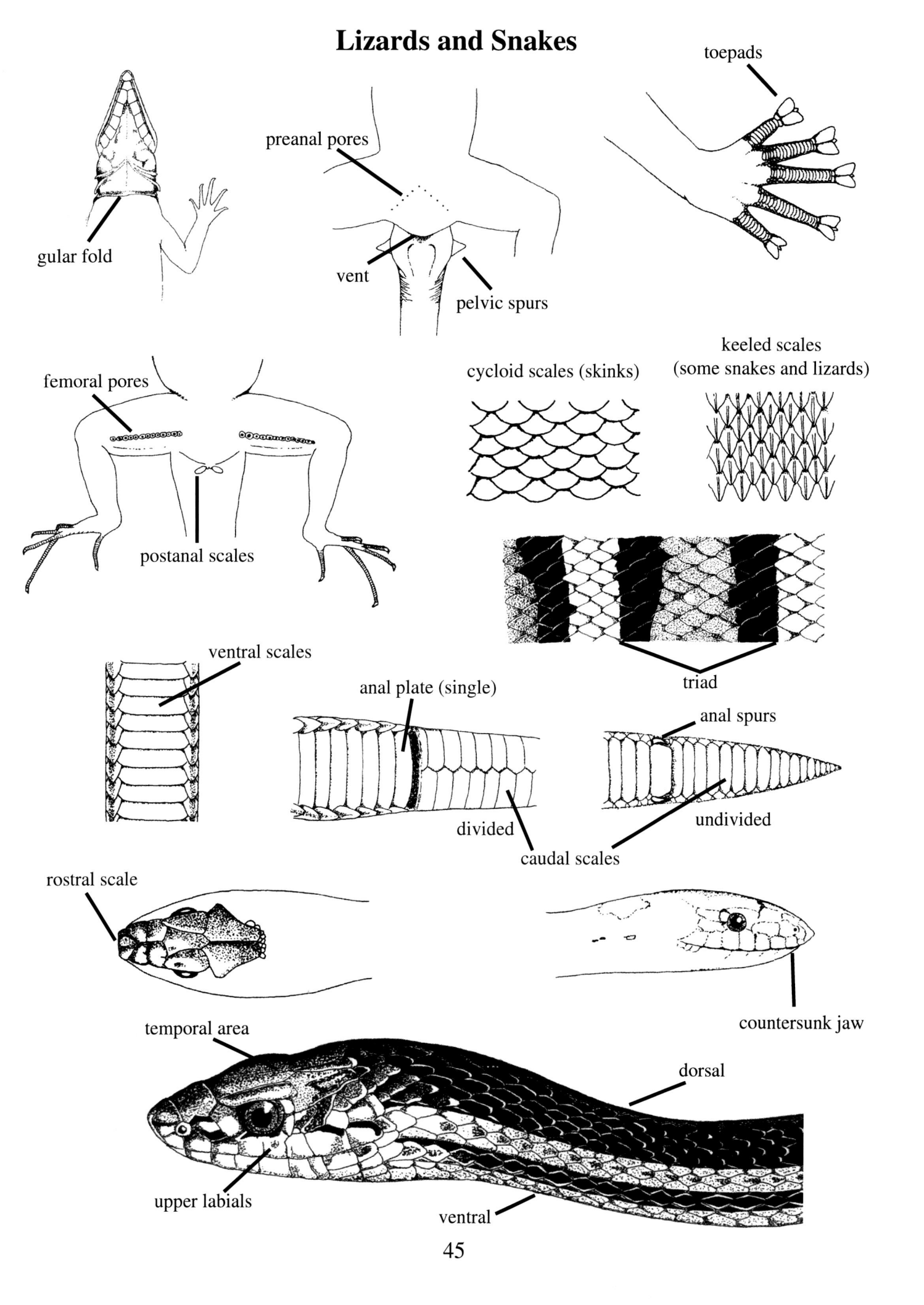

- toepads
- preanal pores
- vent
- pelvic spurs
- gular fold
- femoral pores
- cycloid scales (skinks)
- keeled scales (some snakes and lizards)
- postanal scales
- triad
- ventral scales
- anal plate (single)
- anal spurs
- divided
- undivided
- caudal scales
- rostral scale
- countersunk jaw
- temporal area
- dorsal
- upper labials
- ventral

45

Notes